I0453784

LEARNING
THE SPIRIT OF
THE FOUNDER OF
HAPPY SCIENCE UNIVERSITY

PART I (OVERVIEW)

WHAT IS ACADEMIC DISCIPLINE BASED ON A RELIGIOUS SPIRIT?

Lecture given on August 14, 2014
Inner Shrine Shoja, Happy Science

RYUHO OKAWA
IRH Press

Contents

1

The Reason We Need
Happy Science University
At This Time

2

Happy Science Teachings
Fully Answer the Question,
"What is the Mind?"

Afterword 99

Preface

Now that we aspire to establish the Happy Science University*, we have submitted a statement of our purpose in establishing this and a summary of the curriculum to the Office for University Chartering in the Ministry of Education, Culture, Sports, Science and Technology. Since that time, we have communicated officially twice with their advisory body, known as the Council for University Chartering and School Corporations, and received their response.

As part of this process, we were told by the Council officials that they did not understand the content of the courses, "Learning the Spirit of the Founder" Part I and II, which we are planning to offer as basic liberal arts courses at the Happy Science University. We were also told that they could not evaluate the abilities of the instructor of that course. For these reasons, we were notified that the authorization would be "put on hold."

---

* At the end of October 2014, the Ministry of Education, Culture, Sports, Science and Technology disapproved the establishment of Happy Science University. Although we are calling for the disapproval to be withdrawn, we are planning to open a religious institution for higher education, Happy Science University [HSU] in April 2015.

Sadly, the officials and Council members are not even able to distinguish between "religious leaders" and "scholars of religion." In the first place, they simply say that they "do not understand" because they have not even read any of my books. I do not know which members of the Council this opinion represents. What is more, the Director of the Office for University Chartering in MEXT [Ministry of Education, Culture, Sports, Science and Technology] refused to accept my books when we handed to him, and when we sent them by mail, he simply returned them to us without reading them. Doing this in the screening and consideration process goes beyond a mere lack of research; it amounts to sabotage and a misspending of taxes.

The three officials in charge of this process were "honorably promoted" by Human Affairs as of July 25. And now, all of the explanations and promises made to date seem to be completely up in the air. New officials have come to take their places, but they are now on summer vacation.

Due to all this, I have recently provided an "overview" of the spirit of the founder [Ryuho Okawa] for the people who will try and make the final decision without reading even one of my books, and I have transcribed it as Parts I and II of *Learning the Spirit of the Founder of Happy Science University (Overview)*.

This had an unexpected benefit. It serves even the people who have continued to read the 1,600 plus books that I have written, helping them to grasp my way of thinking from a new angle.

This book, *Learning the Spirit of the Founder Part I*, describes the reasons why a new spiritual pillar is needed in Japan today, as well as my response in relation to the statement from the Council members that they do not understand the "definition of the mind." It also clarifies the core ideas about introducing "spirituality" when it comes to creating a new civilization, which Happy Science University will be undertaking. At the same time, it will also be a new gospel for people who have the desire to study the world of spirituality.

The subject of this book is not just for the establishment of the university. It reveals an unwavering set of guiding principles that will serve as a "North Star" for those aspiring to live in a new era.

Ryuho Okawa
Founder and CEO of Happy Science Group
Founder of Happy Science University
August 16, 2014

This book is based on a discourse given in question-and-answer form.

The two interviewers are denoted as A and B.

1

The Reason We Need
Happy Science University
At This Time

1

The Reason We Need Happy Science University At This Time

QUESTIONER A:

Happy Science University has "studies on happiness" and "the creation of a new civilization" as its founding spirit. Could you please tell us again your vision as the founder, Master Ryuho Okawa, of the founding spirit of Happy Science University, as well as the mission entrusted to Happy Science University?

The postwar regime problem That impacts the whole of Japanese education

RYUHO OKAWA:

In Japan, many universities already exist and when looking at the broader picture, the overall population is declining. While the rate of decline is particularly marked among children and young people, there are quite a lot of universities that are experiencing difficulty in meeting their quota of students. Therefore, if you look at the current situation without taking into account the materials being taught, it is possible to insist that Japan does not need to establish any more new universities. But when it comes to the materials, there is an even bigger problem.

I think this is an issue that impacts the whole of Japanese education. Ever since the postwar Constitution was forced on Japan, constitutional scholars, scholars of civil law, political scientists, and scholars of education who have been stained with left-wing ideological thinking were acclaimed.

To be frank, when the occupying force was setting up the postwar regime, they intentionally created this to weaken Japan. They popularized Communist ideas and those who followed this trend became scholarly leaders, creating different frameworks. Those who are active today are from their pupils' generation or the generation after that.

Meanwhile in politics, the government is undertaking a review of the postwar regime. There have been serious questions from an academic point of view as well, over the issues of Japanese views of history, the Greater East Asia War and the World War II [WWII], where it is believed that Japan's behavior was on a par with the inhumane acts like the holocaust committed by the Nazis.

I am continuously publishing books from the standpoint of a religious leader and from a journalistic point of view in order to inform people of the fact that this statement was simply taken from the anti-war, Japan-bashing propaganda put forth by Japan's enemies at the time.

Nevertheless, education has greater power to nurture the next generation; I believe Japan's education needs a firm backbone.

Education under the Meiji Constitution Had a spiritual pillar

What is the backbone that we need to establish in education? Before the WWII, when the Meiji Constitution [the 1889 Constitution of the Empire of Japan] was in effect, education was based on the spirit of the Meiji Restoration and it reflected the core values of its leaders. Under the Meiji Constitution, State Shintoism generally constituted the spiritual pillar of the nation, centering on the emperor system. From here, a range of moral thinking flowed, which influenced variety of subjects and other academic disciplines.

Of course looking from the perspective of today's "academic freedom" and "diversity," it must have been insufficient in many ways. Since it was a time when Japan was trying to build strength as a newly emerging country in Asia and had the slogan, "enrich the country and strengthen the military," it was indeed true to say that any academic research or philosophies that went against national policy could hardly spread.

Nevertheless, even from the current perspective we can say that nothing inhumane or reactionary that is commonly portrayed by left-wing newspapers and television was taught at the time.

If we look at the Imperial Rescript on Education, too, it beautifully incorporates a *tanka* [31-syllable Japanese poem] in which the Meiji Emperor and Empress expressed the teachings of the mind, as well as the tanka in which the Emperor expressed his own thoughts. In a sense, the art of expressing the Truth in tanka form can be seen the same as the Emperor clarifying thoughts or ideas with religious meanings, and this had a major influence on politics and education, as well as the workings of government. This is what is lacking in the postwar regime.

Shintoism does not meet the criteria For an ordinary religion

I am not trying to argue that the pre-war period was somehow perfect. While the Meiji Constitution enacted freedom of religion and permitted the existence of different religions, the Meiji government maintained the view that State Shintoism — a form of Shintoism based on the Emperor system — was not actually a religion. Shinto was seen as a system of practices and conventions that embodied the traditional values of the Japanese people, as an expression of their customs, habits and cultural traditions.

Simply put, Shinto has long been closely intertwined with traditional customs such as visiting a shrine on New Year's Day to offer prayers and make pledges for the year ahead. For this reason, Shinto was not regarded as a religion in the conventional sense. So, although the Constitution allowed freedom of religion, State Shinto was at the foundation of the nation.

Therefore, Shinto was not a religion in the conventional sense but a system of laws and customs that was the equivalent of the constitution in Japan, prior to the advent of the Meiji Constitution. Shinto was in effect part of the state, a constitution that was created within the context of Japanese history, with the emperor system as the foundation and the structure of government on top of that.

Shinto combined political mechanisms with religious and cultural doctrine. This system of unwritten, undocumented laws survived for a great many years. It was due to this historical background that the government claimed that Shinto was different from other ordinary religions.

The current Religious Corporations Act defines a religion as a movement that has a founder and a basic doctrine or set of beliefs, along with associated ceremonies, rites or protocols, and an organization dedicated to the task of spreading its teachings to the wider public. This is at the basis of the Law.

So a religion must have a founder or guru, and a set of teachings or beliefs. Then it must have ceremonies, rites or protocols. Obviously it also needs buildings of some style in which to conduct these, such as shrines or temples. And it needs some sort of activities to spread its teachings. This can be called missionary work or spreading the message, and these activities always goes with a religion.

Based on this definition, then, traditional Shinto is not considered to be a religion, and the Association of Shinto Shrines formally acknowledges this.

Postwar historians do not admit
The existence of any beings without evidence

It is said that Japanese Shinto has no founder. This is true: there is no figure representing to be the founder of Shinto.

Ancient records such as *Kojiki* [Records of Ancient Matters] and *Nihon-Shoki* [Chronicles of Japan] describe various gods in the mythological age, but in the absence of definitive evidence we have no way of knowing whether they actually existed. We know their names as given in the records, but we do not know their teachings or what they did.

The first emperor appeared at the end of the seventh generation of gods. This was Emperor Jinmu, and since then there has been an unbroken succession of 125 emperors. Historical records exist for most of these emperors except for some of the early ones — specifically, those from the second through to the ninth. There is much debate among historians regarding these particular emperors, including the question of whether or not they actually existed.

For some reason, *Records of Ancient Matters* and *Chronicles of Japan* do not have clear descriptions of these emperors. There are some symbolic references but no definitive information, leading some historians to be skeptical that certain parts of the records might have been made up during the compilation process.

This kind of idea has a close affinity with left-wing materialist and positivist thinking, so among the postwar historians in particular, there is a strong tendency to deny the existence of anything for which there is no evidence.

Emperor Jinmu is generally held to be the first in a long line of emperors. But some historians even claim that someone named Jinmu never existed, and that it was actually Emperor Yuryaku.

Likewise, certain historians even go so far as to argue that the Sun Goddess Amaterasu was not a real being, but was in fact Queen Himiko. Some speculate that Himiko actually lived in either Kyushu or the Yamato region, believing the Himiko theory, while others claim that it was not Himiko at all but rather an historical personage, possibly a reflection of Empress Jingu, who dispatched reinforcements to the Korean peninsula and provided protection to Paekche*, the then ally of Japan.

Another different theory holds that the faith in the Sun Goddess was established to show the orthodoxy of the Empress Jito, who had a direct influence on *Records of Ancient Matters* and *Chronicles of Japan* at the time of their compilation, since a female emperor is utterly unusual. Yet another hypothesis says that the histories may have been rewritten to exaggerate the contributions of Queen Himiko and Empress Jingu.

As long as historians take an evidence-based view of this matter, the further back in time they go, the less certainty they will have about our history.

---

* A kingdom located in what is now southwest Korea [18B.C. - 660A.D.].

The distinctive character of Japanese Shintoism, Whose founder is unknown

So historians are unable to understand who the founder of Japanese Shinto was.

In *Records of Ancient Matters*, Ame-no-Minakanushi-no-Kami [the god who rules the center of heaven] is described as being the very first god to have appeared. It is depicted as a genderless god without a physical body, who suddenly appeared like sky father.

Meanwhile, *Chronicles of Japan* mentions Kuni-no-Tokotachi-no-Kami [the eternal god of the land], but once again there is no clear evidence for his existence. This figure may well have been the first generation or origin of the Imperial Family, signifying the age of the gods, but his thoughts and teachings remain unknown. In other words, it is not clear who the founder of Japanese Shinto was.

Even the Sun Goddess Amaterasu is not the first god, according to the lineage described in *Records of Ancient Matters*. Actually the god Izanagi-no-Mikoto appears in the 12th place. He returned to what is now Miyazaki prefecture in southern Kyushu after holding a funeral for the goddess Izanami-no-Mikoto in the land of the dead [thought to be Izumo][see also Ryuho Okawa, *Izanagi, Izanami no Himitsu ni Semaru* (Tracing the Secrets of Izanagi and Izanami)(Tokyo: IRH Press, 2013)].

After the funeral, Izanagi-no-Mikoto carried out his purification to cleanse the taint of death by washing first his left eye then his right eye, and then he rinsed his nose. In this process, the Three Precious Gods were born, the first of whom was Amaterasu, the Sun Goddess.

Of course, this is intended as a symbolic story and should be interpreted as such. In purely biological terms, the story holds that a child is born when a male god washes his left eye. This is clearly not to be taken literally. For this reason, many scholars, for instance those who insist on evidence, see it as a myth, a parable, a symbolic tale, or a metaphor.

It seems strange that although the Sun Goddess appears later than tenth in the historical lineage of deities, in

Japanese Shinto she is considered to be the highest deity. There is no explanation for this in either *Records of Ancient Matters* or *Chronicles of Japan*.

There are tales of what she did: she had been weaving, she had hidden herself in the rock cave, she had banished her brother Susanoo-no-Mikoto from the country because he tore the horsehide and threw it down from above, breaking the roof. But there is no mention of her overall philosophy or teachings.

There are ceremonial practices for visiting a Shrine, but not teachings

Thus we cannot identify with any certainty the founder of Japanese Shinto, nor do we know the philosophy or teachings. In a sense, Japanese Shinto is like the big red *torii* gate in front of a shrine.

Places of worship in India have stone arches out the front, and I think that these are imitations of the torii gates at Japanese temples. The design of torii gates must have been passed on to India. The shape of the arch is similar to the Chinese character "*ten*" meaning heaven, as used in the names of Ame-no-Minakanushi-no-Kami and Amaterasu. Thus we may conclude that the act of passing beneath a torii gate signifies entering into the world of faith.

While we know the customs of Shinto, we do not clearly know what its teachings are. Some of the teachings are revealed in the books of spiritual messages given by Shinto gods through Happy Science, but in the stream of orthodox Shinto these are not made clear.

In terms of the ceremonies of worship, while there are minor differences between the style at Ise Shrine and Izumo Shrine, all are based on the basic set of order: bowing, putting your hands together and showing respect by clapping.

Prior to this, there is generally a purifying procedure that takes place as the ritual for cleansing earthly taints. At a place for hand washing, you scoop out water with a ladle and wash your mouth and hands to purify yourself before entering the shrine. A typical act of worship involves two sets of bows and two sets of clapping.

So the ceremony takes the basic form of greeting the holy deity, offering a heartfelt prayer and pledge in your mind, then departing. This is all there is in Japanese Shinto and it does not involve any form of religious activities as defined in the aforementioned Religious Corporation Act.

The position of the Association of Shinto Shrines accords with the approach adopted by the Meiji government. People working at the Association of Shinto Shrines themselves also explain that strictly speaking, they are not a religion in the conventional sense, but as they nevertheless have a belief system in a god, they are treated as a religious corporation.

This is the situation today. While Japanese Shinto is no longer the central state religion that it was before the war, it remains as a traditional national religion of Japan, among other religions. And depending on the shrine, there are subtle differences in terms of the deities that are worshipped and the ways of thinking that are adopted.

I want to make Japan a true sovereign state By establishing a new spiritual pillar

The postwar occupation authorities forced Japan to adopt a new constitution, took away the armed forces and prohibited acts of war. Japan was completely stripped of its military forces and has thus started to rebuild itself from a situation where it was virtually no longer a sovereign state. Now that almost seventy years have passed since WWII, I believe that it is time for Japan to restore itself to what a country should essentially be.

For this reason, it is necessary to establish a spiritual pillar in Japan appropriate for the new era. The world religions still remaining to this day include Buddhism, Christianity, and Islam and, in creating a new spiritual pillar we have to learn the important teachings that are contained in them, while at the same time valuing the traditional ways of thinking that are unique to Japan.

And based on this spiritual pillar, we need to set up a new educational system and academic disciplines so that Japan will regain its rightful status as a sovereign state in the near future.

As the first step in Japan rebuilding itself, we need to restore what GHQ [the General Headquarters of the Allied Powers] tried to crush in this country, or create an innovation.

The emperor system itself still remains to this day, but the Imperial Family is only expected to follow formalities and do nothing of substance. So I believe we need some spiritual support in regard to this.

Long ago, Prince Shotoku [574-622] brought Buddhism to Japan on the grounds that the traditional Shinto teachings were insufficient. Buddhism supplemented Shinto with its teachings and created a basic set of the fundamental ways of thinking required of humans, along with academic studies or disciplines, while retaining the traditional ceremonial forms and beliefs in ancient Japanese gods. In this way, Buddhism has flourished in Japan in the syncretism of Shinto and Buddhism.

Happy Science is now trying to introduce a new spiritual philosophy for the current era, the equivalent of the Buddhism that Prince Shotoku brought to Japan, which spread through China and the Korean Peninsula. Based on this new spiritual philosophy, we want to establish a firm principle that is lacking in Japan today, and accomplish what the Meiji Restoration did not completely achieve.

Taisho and Showa era
Lost the spirit of the Meiji era

During the Meiji Restoration, people's stance changed from supporting the idea of "expelling foreigners" to the "opening of Japan," which brought about the Westernization of the Japanese diet and lifestyle. At the same time, though, there was also an idea of supporting the restoration of imperial rule, which urged the Tokugawa Shogunate to return political power to the Emperor. So the Meiji Restoration was in fact combined with the idea of returning to old times.

In Europe, meanwhile, the French Revolution occurred, which eventually led to the imperial rule of Napoleon, then to the return of the monarchy once more. In England, Oliver Cromwell led the Puritan Revolution in which he executed the king, but there was a backlash against the severity of his regime, which in turn sparked the Glorious Revolution and the restoration of the monarchy again.

In the same way, the Meiji Restoration was accompanied by a return to the old ways to some degree, as well as opening up a new phase. So the Meiji government integrated both the new ways and the old ways in their administration.

While the leaders of the Meiji Restoration and the elder statesmen, who had made an outstanding contribution to the Restoration and who embodied the Meiji spirit, were still active, they gave their interpretation of the various areas where guiding principles were lacking, and thus the government ran smoothly.

However, after these elder statesmen passed away one after another, during the Taisho era and the beginning of Showa era, Japan no longer had sufficient new guiding principles for the nation. This lack of leadership was then exposed in the WWII, and brought tremendous suffering and loss to the people of Japan.

The necessity of Happy Science University In the context of the current state Of religious universities

If you look around the world today, you will see that, notwithstanding a few exceptions, religion exists in nearly all the countries of the world. Over ninety percent of countries embrace religion in some form or another, and this is reflected in their ways of thinking and their approach to academic disciplines.

Japan is something of an exception; while it imitates the American way of thinking, it has not adopted the Christian spirit of the Americans sufficiently in its academic disciplines. During WWII in Japan, Christianity was considered heretical, much like Communism, and was often subject to suppression.

After the war Christianity revived in Japan, but it tended to be closely aligned with left-wing ideologies and what Communism and Christianity say is almost the same. Both have been repressed in the past, and therefore tend to regard the state as a malevolent force.

After the war, the GHQ intentionally encouraged left-wing movements in Japan for a certain period of time. And, while there are a number of Christian universities in Japan, due to the repression suffered during the war, ideas similar to those in left-wing movements underlie these universities as well. Therefore, the education these universities are providing is not necessarily based on pure Christian teachings, unlike in the U.S.

Christianity has entered Japan as some kind of an "anti-state religion," so ideologies that oppose the state have secretly been infiltrating many Christian universities in Japan. This does not apply to all of the Christian universities in Japan, but it is true to many of them.

Japan also has Buddhist universities, but in these universities too, the content of academic disciplines has lost the essence in the course of over 2,500 years of Buddhist history. Buddhism has changed since Shakyamuni Buddha's era, when it has pursued the attainment of enlightenment to a place where the nature of enlightenment itself is now unclear.

Since the Kamakura era [1185-1333], Buddhist sects have moved towards "competition for benefit," where they only pursue what brings tangible benefits in this world, as well as the expansion of movements based on simplistic slogans.

For example, some sects teach that you will be saved by just chanting "namu-amida-butsu" [Homage to Amitabha Buddha] or by just chanting "namu-mhyoho-renge-kyo" [Homage to the Lotus Sutra], while others only focus on the practice of Zen meditation. However, I must say that they all fall short of the fundamental spirit of Buddhism.

Thus, from a completely new standpoint, we need to establish a new organization that is dedicated to long-term research and the elaboration of ideals that can create a nation for the coming era, along with a new type of education and talented people, while also incorporating a religious spirit. This is why I believe that Happy Science University is now required.

I want Happy Science University to be An advanced educational institution That exports new academic disciplines

Happy Science University will, of course, adopt Japanese traditions and the best elements from other countries. It will not support the simplistic scientific denials that seem to be a feature of many religions, but will adopt a scientific approach as well. At the same time it will also incorporate a wide range of other academic disciplines.

Happy Science University will also adopt the good aspects of other religions and will learn from their strong points. While it has its own religion, Happy Science, as the backdrop, it also has the attitude of studying and absorbing the good that is to be found in other religions.

In this sense, I intend to reconstruct philosophies and ways of thinking anew to create a new Japanese philosophy, invent a new academic discipline that has originated in Japan, and then export it to the rest of the world. To achieve this end, I want to create Happy Science University as an advanced, state-of-the-art institution.

This being so, if we are forced to create the same sort of institution as the existing universities, then unfortunately it is not right to attempt to build a university by collecting offerings from our followers.

Acquiring new believers is not the purpose Of building Happy Science University

Every individual has the freedom to choose which university he or she wants to attend, so basically there will be no compulsion involved in opening a university. And certainly, we are not setting up a university with the intention of creating new believers of Happy Science.

In fact, I would say it is rather the Christian sects that seem to be trying to build universities in order to create new believers. In their universities, about half of their students at most are the children of believers, irrespective of whether the children themselves have a faith. Thus, the teaching staff including professors, associate professors, and lecturers, can include non-Christians.

In order to survive, they remain flexible on this point. Maybe they are only aiming at the level where students gain a basic appreciation of Christianity just by attending their university, a level equivalent to Tenrikyo's *nioigake*, or feeling the spirit of Tenrikyo. I suppose they are satisfied with that degree of influence.

The nation's "right to know" And "right to learn" must be secured

Christianity has a five-hundred year history of missionary work in Japan, yet Christians account for less than one percent of the total population of Japan, their numbers not even reaching one million.

According to insiders, officially there would be around one million Christians, but others say that even if all the different sects and strands of Christianity practicing in Japan were brought together, the actual number of believers would be no more than about 600,000 in total.

I do not know the exact number of Christian universities operating in Japan, but I imagine there would not be just five or ten of them, but many more. That means that all these universities are licensed to operate for the benefit of barely 600,000 believers who represent less than one percent of the total population of Japan.

In contrast, Happy Science is now steadily growing in popularity, carrying into the hearts of many, many more people in Japan. There are Japanese citizens who take an interest in this new belief system and in learning its teachings, and who have a desire to study them. But if there were nowhere they could exercise their right to learn or their right to know, that would be really unfortunate.

There are things to learn at each level in the academic world. Besides, it is true to say that over-competitive entrance examinations have brought about the situation where students' minds become disturbed, families fracture and society is dysfunctional. Therefore, it is necessary to offer a dose of "coolant" and circulate a breath of fresh air through Japan's high-stress, over-competitive society.

To achieve that, a university with a religious backbone that upholds the ideals of cherishing, loving, and helping one another, is essential.

In any case, a nation's right to know, or the right to study of those who have faith, must be secured without being persecuted. For these are the fundamental rights of the people.

A university for a new era that provides Study opportunities for religious people

People with a religious faith may attend a Christian university or one of the universities associated with the older Buddhist sects, such as Komazawa University and Rissho University. Unfortunately, however, when those who adhere to the beliefs of Happy Science attend one of these universities, they still feel quite uncomfortable due to the differences in their beliefs.

For example, Sophia University is a Christian university in Japan, but even that university has signs prohibiting any missionary activities on campus. Sophia University is based on the Catholic Jesuit order, so presumably these signs mean that other religions are not approved of. Thus it allows no religious freedom on campus and approves of only one religion. For this reason, other religions cannot do missionary work in that university.

Another example is Keio University, founded by Yukichi Fukuzawa [1835-1901]. In his writing entitled *Fukuo Jiden* [An Autobiography of Fukuzawa Yukichi], he makes light of religion and claims that it has no place in the age of enlightenment. Fukuzawa pokes fun at the worship of *Inari* [god of the harvest], boasting that he once opened up an Inari shrine to find that the object of worship inside was just a single stone, which he threw away and replaced with another.

But afterwards no curse was visited upon him for committing this act. Fukuzawa describes this story as one of his heroic episodes or boasts. But I am afraid that those who study such a story may develop a tendency to view religion as no more than praying to a stone.

Along the same lines, there are many people who understand religions in a shallow way. As the old Japanese saying goes, even the head of a sardine can be a charm against evil if you believe in it; people think that anyone can create a religion simply by successfully making people believe in whatever is set out before them.

So, creating a new system of academic disciplines while incorporating into it a completely genuine religious spirit is a tremendous venture. But I believe this is something absolutely necessary, as a whole new paradigm.

There is a real need in society now to create educational institutions suited for the new age that can deliver a university education, while accepting people who believe in a religion with religious tolerance and people with a religious character. And I believe that it is our duty to fulfill this need.

2

Happy Science Teachings Fully Answer the Question, "What is the Mind?"

2

Happy Science Teachings Fully Answer the Question, "What is the Mind?"

QUESTIONER B:

On the subject of Happy Science University, you state in your book entitled *The New Idea of a University* [see Figure 1] that the university will be a "source of a new civilization." And in the *Prayer for Great Success in Establishing Happy Science University*, you also state that it will be "the womb of all life on earth." Please tell us about the role of Happy Science University in creating a new civilization.

Figure 1.
Ryuho Okawa, *The New Idea of a University: The Groundbreaking Mission of Happy Science University* (New York: IRH Press, 2014).

The interesting thing in the opinion
We received back from the Council

RYUHO OKAWA:

Well, this is related to religious matters so it is a bit sensitive, but what happened was this: We applied to the government for permission to establish a university, and as part of this process, we submitted documents to the Ministry of Education, Culture, Sports, Science and Technology. They had discussions with officials such as the Council regarding establishing the university, and twice we received feedback after their review. Reading that feedback, we noticed something interesting from our point of view.

For example, one of the faculties that we are planning to offer is a field of science called the "Faculty of Future Industry," and the related documents submitted by Happy Science University use the word "mind" quite often. The feedback we received about this was that, "because there is no academic basis to the word 'mind,' a word of this sort should not be used in a science-oriented field of study."

This alone made me realize that for the review of a religious university, we are dealing with people who are really difficult.

Exploring "material things" will not lead you to Discovering "the mind"

They are asking, "what is 'the mind'," and specifically to answer this, I would say that it is "in contrast to a physical object." In other words, to answer the question, "What is the mind?" a general description would be "something that is psychological, not physical." And specifically it can be described as, "that which can be defined as 'the psychological processes of human beings'."

It is fine to study science as a "materialistic academic field." However, if people only explore this and do not accept other aspects like personal beliefs and views on life, philosophical views, "faith" and "spiritual view of life" in everyday living, then in the end, they are only exploring "physical objects."

In the Faculty of Engineering, people focus only on the functioning of machines. In faculties related to chemistry, people only do research into subjects like chemical reactions and changes. Or the same goes to the Faculty of Medicine, they think of the human as a simple machine, and believe that hospital merely fulfills the role of an "automobile maintenance facility," which just takes apart, reassembles, and repairs machines. However, no matter how much they explore "physical objects," they will not be able to discover "the mind."

There are people who have a worldview that this earth is only a "world of objects" or a "materialistic world." They believe the main aim of academic studies is the materialistic world and think the world where we can see and touch is everything. For these people, what I call "the mind" is simply one function of the brain.

In other words, they perceive "the mind" only as a function of the frontal, temporal, and occipital lobes, or as a function of some part of the cerebral cortex. And they say things like, "When we applied an electrical stimulus there, 'this kind of reaction occurred' or 'this kind of memory surfaced'." I believe that this is a type of thinking which conceptually reduces humans to mere robots or cyborgs.

In this way, their way of thinking is along the lines of, "If 'the mind' is a function of the brain or the nervous system, then I can understand it," or, "If you can record it as data, then you can call it 'the mind,' but if there is something that you cannot record as data, something you cannot measure, then it is not 'the mind'."

Furthermore, when it comes to matters like emotions as well, they understand them in terms such as, "Emotions arise when a variety of reactions occur in the body, for instance when the internal secretion of chemicals like adrenaline occurs, the body temperature alters, the blood pressure changes, or the blood flow in the physical heart or the brain changes."

The teachings of world religions are Well established as an academic subject

For people who imagine the limits of "the mind" only at this level, subjects like the enlightenment of the Buddha or the Christian teachings of Jesus, for example, must make absolutely no sense. They probably feel as if it is all nonsense.

The Buddha says, "If you renounce the world and engage in religious training, you will achieve enlightenment. And you will enter Nirvana." In other words, this teaching means that after your physical body perishes, you can return to a place of rest.

To people who try to explore the mind on the basis that humans are like a machine, this Buddhist teaching is nothing more than superstitious belief. They see it as a primitive way of thinking.

On the other hand, let us take a look at the concept of resurrection, spoken of in Christianity. Jesus was crucified on the cross, but afterwards he was resurrected, proving that human beings are spiritual beings, then returned to the place where God is.

There is a belief, "Jesus Christ was reborn into this world from the heavenly realm to save humankind. He lived out his life for 33 years, spent his last three years ardently devoted to missionary work, was crucified on the cross, and returned to Heaven.

But, even though his physical body died, his soul lives on forever, striving to save people." However, to those who look at things from a materialistic, science-oriented perspective, the entire story lacks evidence. There is absolutely no proof.

And yet, if you doubt that this could ever be a field of academic study, you would be wrong, because it does in fact exist as a scholarly subject. Basically, materialists look only at "physical objects" and do not understand "the mind." So they think that everything exists in physical objects, and that the whole world exists at the physical level.

This is like looking at "a drop of water as a universe." It is a viewpoint where they look at a drop of water through a microscope, seeing all of the various small microscopic organisms that live within it, and claiming, "this is the world."

On the other hand, the people who look at the "world of the mind" are able to see a world beyond what is visible through a microscope. Or, conversely, you could say that these people are looking into the depths of the universe through a telescope. The point is, however, that there are people who do not know of the existence of that vast world.

In any case, "the mind" exists as something that is in direct contrast to "physical objects."

*The deep psyche appeared
As something against materialism*

People who claim that it is impossible to define "the mind," or that "mind" is something incomprehensible, can by and large be thought of as materialists. On the other hand, those who have researched subjects such as religion, other spiritual philosophies, or certain types of psychology, generally understand that the mind is not all about what we are able to perceive outwardly.

For example, in the field of psychology, in the work of people like Jung [1875-1961] and Freud [1856-1939] we find "depth psychology." The idea is that there is a deep layer of the psyche outside of the conscious part that appears on the surface, and it is called the deep psyche. This deep psyche is a form of awareness that is normally dormant, but in actuality has a major effect on our tendencies. It creates the drama in our lives, and is a most important factor in constructing our destiny.

By exploring the deep psyche, people can clarify what the various frustrations, discord, and anxieties, which arise in their lives, really represent. As a result, they can resolve those problems, turn their lives around for the better, and even be able to return to a workplace they have previously left. This kind of approach is used in the field of psychology.

So, even in the academic field of current psychology encompasses the idea that the human mind is more than just the physical reactions within a brain and nerves, the idea that "a layer of consciousness that is not perceivable on the surface, called the deep psyche, actually exists," is largely acknowledged and accepted.

Nevertheless, the definitions of what this concept means are still not entirely sufficient. In actuality, it is rather difficult to explain without relying on religion. But still, the concept is recognized to a large extent.

The discovery of the deep psyche was one of the discoveries of the twentieth century. In the late nineteenth century, perhaps the materialism of Marx and Engels can also be regarded as one discovery from that era; the deep psyche was also discovered simultaneously by the likes of Freud and Jung, so that it could serve to counter materialism as a movement in the opposite direction.

Humanities cannot be established without Understanding "the mind"

I have just stated that the mind is something that is in direct contrast to physical objects. So the question then would be, "What exactly is the mind?" Of course, the term "the mind" has multiple meanings. In order to illustrate the fact that there are some things, which cannot be expressed only through physical objects, let me give you an example that is a little easier to comprehend.

Try, for example, to explain the phrase, "the thousand-year old spirit of Kyoto," from the perspective of material sciences. If someone were to ask you, "What does the thousand-year old spirit of Kyoto mean?" how would you answer?

Most people would be limited to responses that referred to architectural structures such as, "Here is a five-storied pagoda," "Here is the Tenryuji Temple, "Here is the Yasaka Shrine." And they would say things like, "The impression you get from those types of buildings is the thousand-year old spirit of Kyoto."

But the truth is that the phrase, "the thousand-year old spirit of Kyoto," contains many different meanings that are much, much deeper. I feel that this phrase reflects all sorts of thoughts and feelings of the Japanese people that have been portrayed in history. In this way, what we call "the spirit" or "the mind" can be used as a general term that applies to the mental processes and emotions of people, things which cannot be expressed in physical terms alone.

Or, if we look at terminology that has been around for ages, we have the phrase, "the heart of *Yamato*." "The heart of Yamato" is a phrase that is absolutely incomprehensible in materialistic terms. This sort of term is completely impossible to explain materialistically. If materialistic people were asked, "What is the heart of Yamato?" the question would be utterly unanswerable for them.

If you want to know what the heart of Yamato is, you must learn about the history of the Japanese people and about the spirit of great historical figures, those spiritual pioneers who wove patterns of thoughts or gave religious teachings. Unless you do this, you will not be able to understand what we call "the heart of Yamato," and even if someone tells you about "the heart of *Mahoroba* [the blissful land of Japan]," you will not be able to grasp it.

Being unable to understand these abstract concepts [mind, spirit, or heart] illustrates that there are limits to the materialistic worldview, and materialistic people must accept this fact. If you are to think and perceive only in a materialistic way, then basically anything that is to do with the humanities cannot be accepted as academic study in universities.

I understand "the humanities" to be a general term used to describe the scientific and research-oriented approach to culture that humans have created. A materialistic foundation would not allow those sorts of fields to exist as areas of study. This is also true for social sciences, though I would not say about the entire field of social sciences.

After all, as long as you believe that you can only think of the world in materialistic terms, or analytically, you cannot understand any abstract concepts. However, even the principles of modern politics are basically abstract concepts.

Specifically, there is a building called the National Diet [Japanese Government], and the political principles that are enacted within it, such as "the separation of the three powers," "majority rule," and, "the Constitution takes precedence over the law," are ultimately not entirely concrete after all. In fact, they are made up of conceptual and intangible elements to a large extent.

Therefore, anyone who cannot comprehend abstract thought would fundamentally not be able to understand subjects like social sciences, or the study of the law, political science, or the study of economics.

What are the preconceptions
In the study of economics?

Furthermore, even in the study of economics, people like to assert that you can perform quantitative analysis as if it were a science. But in most cases, what happens is that the analyst presupposes the existence of an "economic human," or "homo economicus," and then merely hypothesizes how he will act in a specific instance.

That is to say, there is an idea that the economic human will determine a course of action based on perceived gains and losses, and act rationally, and the field of microeconomics is basically founded on this way of thinking. In the field of macroeconomics, analysis is conducted based on the idea that, overall, gatherings of these kinds of individuals will act in the same rational way in certain kinds of situations.

However, from a religious perspective I must say that the study of economics itself has some kind of "faith." It contains a great deal of dogma, and a great number of assertions and preconceptions. There is no definite proof that this "homo economicus" type of person exists. And people frequently act in ways that do not correspond to economic principles.

For example, the rate of savings in Japan is extremely high, with some 1.5 quadrillion yen in savings accumulated in the private sector. The government debt is about 1 quadrillion yen, which means that the private sector still has 0.5 quadrillion yen more in savings and bonds than the amount of national debt.

Thus, if you look at the nation as a "conglomerate of citizens," overall Japan is in the black, to the tune of about 0.5 quadrillion yen. Thus, there is basically no way the nation can crumble economically.

What could crumble would merely be the organization that we call "the government." It could possibly go too far into the red and wind up being streamlined, with the merging and closing down of some government offices. But the actual country of Japan itself will basically never crumble.

So, what would the government do to get out of this 1 quadrillion yen debt in national finances? If the government encourages the people to use their 1.5 quadrillion yen capital as much as possible and successfully creates a spending boom, the economy will grow. If companies profit, incomes will increase, and so will the resultant tax revenue. And if tax revenue increases, incoming money will increase, and the country will be able to pay back its debt. In this way, the government will be able to reduce their debt.

Thinking in this way, the government takes the lead on this and, at the same time, tries to pass a law to increase consumption tax as well. If the people spend lots of money and buy lots of goods, and the tax rate also increases further, the government will be able to expect a "multiplied" increase in taxes and obviously, the tax revenue collected by the government will increase.

If the tax rate increases from 5% to 8%, then from 8% to 10%, and yet again from 10% to 16%, as long as everyone keeps purchasing goods, the total revenue from tax will increase even further. Strangely however, "homo economicus" often follows an intuitive line of action.

The government thinks, "If the financial deficit of the government decreases and our debt is reduced, trust in our nation will increase, and trust by foreign powers will also increase, so we will be able to attract investments from other countries. And as a country, we can promote our stability in terms of our national debt, so we would also receive a higher ranking from international financial institutions. Nothing but good would come of this."

But in reality, if the consumption tax rate increased, individuals and households, as "homo economicus," would follow their natural instincts and tighten their purse strings.

Basically, people would stop purchasing as many goods if they had to pay extra taxes on their purchases, so actually, a consumption tax rate increase would not link to an increase in revenue for the government. The government is trying to make people use their capital, but what it ends up doing is exactly the opposite.

It appears to be heading in a direction which leads people not to spend their money, making them believe, "We need to be frugal and save money since the future looks alarming." From this we can see that people do not necessarily behave according to the logic used in academic fields.

All academic fields cannot function If it ignores "the mind"

Thinking in terms of Marx's *Das Kapital* [Capital], some people believe that when individuals compete in a free market and acquire capital, resulting in the production of capitalists, then it will produce strong people and weak people. When this happens, eventually the strong will win, and the society will consist of the weak being ruled by the strong.

Eventually a great panic will take hold, and capitalism will fail. Events like the global panic of 1929 appeared to be examples of that phenomenon occurring, and some people most probably thought, "Marx was right after all."

In recent times, we have seen the "Lehman Shock" in 2008. Based on mathematical formulas, Nobel Prize recipients put together a new American financial product, in which debt was taken apart and combined with all sorts of elements so that the original debt itself became untraceable, and no one could tell which portion of the debt went to who. The compartmentalized portions of the debt were then sold off, and scattered far and wide so that the original debt was completely ungraspable. But ultimately, in the end, debt is debt, and even when it is divided up, combined, and sold, that does not mean that capital has increased.

So, basically what happened was an act equivalent to what we in Japan call "stock shuffling" by the securities companies and banks, but the debt was hidden under even more complex layers of theory and mathematics, and essentially reassembled as products in ways that were so multifarious as to defy detection. And this is what caused immense panic.

It is said that as many as three Nobel Prize winning scholars in the area of economics were involved, so the

Nobel Prize has somewhat lost its dignity. Their theory has actually collapsed. What we experienced was the truth that ultimately, the inflation of imaginary money that does not conform to actual economics will never succeed.

However, even this did not really mean the "end of the world." We did enter a temporary recession, but if we start over and rebuild, we can return to the way things were.

So, in the study of economics, as well as in other areas such as legal studies, political science, and social sciences, it is necessary to know that if you do not look at some form of mental processes or the way the human mind moves, then ultimately, even the social sciences cannot function as an academic field. Neither the humanities nor the social sciences can have any validity if they completely ignore the mind.

Therefore, you simply cannot say that because there is no definition of the mind, there is no such thing as "the mind." While this statement sounds like a Zen riddle, it does not work to say, "If there is no definition of the mind, there is no mind."

The mind at the level of ethics must contain The wisdom to differentiate good from evil

So, what exactly is "the mind" after all? In the final analysis, we must turn to religion for the answer, but I must also state here that no matter how much scholars deny the existence of "the mind" academically, to a certain extent all people in the world commonly accept that humans have a mind.

And, speaking in a primitive way, if we approach this question from the very simplest religious perspective, we can say that a person's mind is what contains the wisdom to differentiate between good and evil.

In this world, we understand what is right to do and what is wrong to do, what we should proceed with, and what we should not proceed with, and we make judgments appropriate to our age. So first of all, I could say that the mind is the mental function that judges between good and evil. This is the mind at the level of ethics.

The mental energy called "the soul"
Is the basis for the existence of the mind
At the religious level

If you raise your argument to the religious level, what would "the mind" mean? Certainly, religion acknowledges the existence of the soul. Generally speaking, the soul is something like an "etheric body" in a human shape that fits inside our own body, and is almost the same shape as a human with a physical body. This kind of spiritual energy, mental energy, or energy body resides in our physical body.

When a living person becomes a dead body, that person stops moving altogether. In physical terms, there is no change, and yet there is a difference between life and death. The reason why there is a difference between life and death is that, ultimately, the substance of a person's energy for activity ceases to exist. And when the substance of energy for activity no longer exists, that means that something has left.

In terms of a machine, it could be compared to the batteries going flat. In terms of a car, you could compare it to the gasoline being all used up. But, in any case, what has happened is that something, which amounts to the "energy source" for a human being's life activity has dissipated.

Having said this, the energy source that is produced in order for us to maintain our life activity is, generally, food. As long as we drink water and eat food, humans are able to continue to live as organisms that have bodies like those of animals. However, once a person dies and becomes a dead body, he can no longer move, even if you give him food or water. He will not move even if you insert an IV drip.

Interpreting this simply as "the brain function has ceased" is the norm in modern medical science. But in order to prove that idea wrong, I have published over 270 books in my "spiritual messages book series" in the last five years. The spiritual beings that appear in the spiritual messages book series are all beings whose bodies have been cremated so clearly, they have no skull or gray matter. That is to say, they do not have any physical brain. They have no frontal lobes, no temporal lobes.

The brain has been analyzed and spoken of as, for example, "the left side of the brain handles calculations and languages," or, "the right side handles imaging," and, "we possess the ability to think deeply in the frontal lobe." All of this amounts to the medical opinion that, "if people did not have brains, they could not think at all."

However, in truth, even after being cremated and when nothing physical remains, people still retain their own individuality after death, and they still have the power to think. Proving this is actually one of the functions of my spiritual messages book series.

In a sense, my spiritual messages book series is "Scientific proof"

I feel that in a sense, this series serves as scientific proof. In the past, many religions have taught of the existence of the other world, and the existence of the soul and the spirit, or taught that human beings are spiritual entities. But it is true to say that it has been very difficult to actually prove through repeated experiments that the soul and spirit do, in fact, really exist. Therefore, whether people believe this or not has been a "test of faith" that asks whether they choose to believe in the teachings of the founders of religions, or choose to believe in the teachings of philosophers.

But now, by calling forth the spirits of a variety of individuals who once possessed physical bodies and individuality, and introducing their words in my series of books of spiritual messages, I have actually been successful in carrying out "repeated experiments." And, through this, I have come to understand that as an individual, each entity has a different way of thinking, and that even though they do not have a physical body or a brain, putting aside their experiences in the Spirit World, they can put forward ways of thinking that are almost the same as the unique way they thought while they were still alive.

For example, whenever I called forth the spirit of Konosuke Matsushita, the founder of Panasonic, he would give his thoughts in a manner worthy of the title, "the god of management," which matched his business-oriented thinking when he was alive. Or, when I call forth the spirit of a certain Buddhist monk, he would give his thoughts in a manner very similar to the way that monk used to think.

So, I have summoned some several hundred spirits of people who belonged to many different "genres" during their lives, from the distant past to the recently deceased. And by continuing to put their words out in books, those books are now recognized to the extent that they are authorized as the content for advertisements in national newspapers in Japan.

The significance of having full-page spread Advertisements for my spiritual messages Book series in national newspapers

This very day on which I am speaking, August 14, 2014, just happens to be the day before the Memorial Day for the End of the WWII. And looking at the *Sankei Shimbun* newspaper today, I found a full-page spread advertisement for our spiritual messages book series. The advertisement also includes information on my book entitled *The Secret Behind "The Rape of Nanking": A Spiritual Confession by Iris Chang* [see Figure 2]. [Another full-page spread advertisement was printed in the *Yomiyuri Shimbun* newspaper the next day, on August 15th, as well.]

Figure 2.
Ryuho Okawa, *The Secret Behind "The Rape of Nanking": A Spiritual Confession by Iris Chang* (New York: IRH Press, 2014).

Iris Chang published the book *The Rape of Nanking* in 1997. This book asserted that, in the last World War, Japanese forces engaged in a giant massacre of around three hundred thousand people in Nanking.

It also claimed that, furthermore, Japanese troops forcibly took women from the Korean peninsula and other areas, and pressed them into service for the troops. These women were called, "military comfort women," but were purported to be basically "sex slaves." The Japanese forces are said in this book to have allegedly committed the inhuman act of enslaving these women.

The book *The Rape of Nanking* sold around five hundred thousand copies in the U.S., becoming a best seller. This means that a percentage of the American public has been poisoned by this book. It was also widely used in the Anti-Japan Campaigns of China and South Korea.

On the other hand, a variety of newspapers provide evidence from different sources that show this kind of incident never really happened. And finally, in the messages from the spirit of Iris Chang, we posed the question to her, "Can you swear to Heaven that the Nanking Massacre actually happened?" That question became the name of the book [note: the English title is *The Secret Behind "The Rape of Nanking": A Spiritual Confession by Iris Chang*], and now that name is being printed in full-page spread advertisements in newspapers all over Japan. This means that we now have enough social standing to have newspapers run advertisements for this book without having to be concerned that people will think of it as delusion, lies, or fraud.

Iris Chang passed away some ten years ago. When I called forth her spirit and conducted a spiritual interview with her, she basically said, "There were numerous errors in my book. There were errors in my checking of facts. I was fed information from all sorts of American and Chinese organizations that made me write it. I did not commit suicide. I was assassinated."

And in the full-page spread newspaper advertisement for this book included the opinions of various scholars who agree with this. From this you can see that these kinds of spiritual messages are becoming more and more accepted by society.

Currently, I am trying to prove that spiritual entities exist. But since so much written material exists, that alone is sufficient for it to be treated as a field of academic research. In the field of religious studies, for example, if there are over 270 books in a spiritual messages book series, I believe that they are worth treating as a subject of academic research.

Various religions became the subject of Research simply because a large amount of Material existed

There have been similar cases in the past as well. For example, there is the case of Emanuel Swedenborg, a Swedish man who lived in the days of Kant. He had the power of spiritual sight or clairvoyance, out of body experiences, and astral travel, and witnessed Heaven and Hell. He wrote massive amounts of text about the Heavenly plane and Hell, and the entire collection of his writings is available for reading.

Emanuel Swedenborg's church has given rise to a valid religion, or religious sect. And in fact, the famous deaf and blind Helen Keller was actually devoted to the religion taught by Emanuel Swedenborg, which is basically categorized as a denomination of Christianity.

So there are people like this, and what I would like to say here is that, ultimately, once the materials exceed a certain quantity, then those materials do become a valid subject of research.

Also, as a recent figure, there was Sathya Sai Baba of India who passed away a few years ago. Though I do not have the confidence to affirm for the authenticity of his conduct, he allegedly performed many different "miracles." He healed the sick and performed many other "miracles." In addition to that, he built schools, hospitals, and even established a university. He even went so far as to feature on a postage stamp in India.

As a religious organization, his teachings had a following of approximately three hundred thousand people. Many people came to visit India from all over the world. And from donations he built many institutions like hospitals and schools. So we can see that when it comes to the field of religion even a modern figure can be the subject of a postage stamp and can build hospitals, schools, and universities.

There is also the religion known as Mormonism, which has teachings that were suppressed in the U.S. in the 1800s as "heretical." This religion originated in New York, but after being persecuted, the adherents followed in the footsteps of Moses on his Exodus, crossing the Rocky Mountains and finally settling in Salt Lake City in the state of Utah.

After this, they created a Mormon settlement, and the followers still live in and around that area. Recently, a Mormon went so far as to stand as a Presidential candidate for the Republican Party in the U.S., so we can see that the religion has achieved a certain social status.

Moreover, in Utah, there is even the Brigham Young University founded by Brigham Young, the second founding leader of Mormonism. In fact, one of the graduates from this new religious-based university has come to Japan and appears in an NHK [Japan Broadcasting Corporation] English conversation class. This is a perfect example of tolerance.

Mormon missionaries are fluent in Japanese, so they appear and give their opinions on different kinds of television shows, as one way of doing their missionary work. Even among new religions there are groups that do this sort of thing.

In religion, "an increase in believers" takes The place of established proof

In religion, proving the existence of the soul and the existence of the other world is an extremely difficult endeavor. And it is true that religions have not been able to offer "proof" through scientific experiment. After all, being recognized as a credible social force in a democratic sense, through the process of an increase in the number of people who believe in the word of God, or the word of prophets, has been a component of religious missionary work.

If the number of people who believe in a religion grows beyond a certain size, the belief is recognized as a having a credible "social standing" and being a valid "force." It then becomes interpreted as one valid way of thought, creed, opinion, or ideology of the people. And it is this kind of sentiment that drives everyone to devote themselves passionately to missionary work.

If the number of believers reaches several hundred thousand, or several million, the religion becomes a solid social power or becomes able to engage in political activities. If the number of believers is counted in the hundred millions, then it can go on to become a world religion.

Fundamentally, because you cannot prove directly, saying, "believe in this," and gathering a certain number of believers produce results similar to having people sign petitions or casting votes. And this exists instead of proof.

When the number of people who believe the messages of the founder of a religion or a great master of a faith rises to a certain level, there is no choice but to recognize their social credibility. For example, if there are as many as three hundred thousand followers, which incidentally is about the same number of people allegedly killed in the great Nanking Massacre [which is actually a fabrication], then it would be unforgivable to say, "all of those people are insane, so we should slaughter them all."

If three hundred thousand believers exist, enough people to fill one large city, then society must recognize that their viewpoint exists, and what they believe in will take form. The teachings of God will take form. This is how religions prove things.

Happy Science explores the secrets of The Spirit World and the soul

In the case of Happy Science, we increase the number of believers through missionary work as an act of faith and we publish many books. In addition to that, we also explore the Spirit World.

As detailed in the Trilogy of our basic teachings, *The Laws of the Sun*, *The Golden Laws*, and *The Nine Dimensions* [see Figure 3], the various religions, philosophies, and fundamental ideologies that arose in different places all over the world all originated from God and Buddha. These books explain how they originated, and describe in separate sections how there are a variety of different ideologies, in terms of levels and types. And, the books also explore the truth about the Spirit World.

Of course, it is possible to approach these solely from the question of "choosing to believe or not to believe," and the messages of these books will probably not reach the hearts of people who only see the world in terms

Figure 3.

Ryuho Okawa, *The Laws of the Sun: One Source, One Planet, One People* (New York: IRH Press, 2013).

Ryuho Okawa, *The Golden Laws: History through the Eyes of the Eternal Buddha* (New York: Lantern Books, 2011).

Ryuho Okawa, *The Nine Dimensions: Unveiling the Laws of Eternity* (New York: IRH Press, 2012).

of physical objects. However, even among scientists, engineers, and scholars in scientific fields, there are many who recognize these messages as having a theoretical consistency, and there are many faithful followers who believe in them.

In fact, there are a large number of believers from the scientific fields in Happy Science, and many university professors and medical doctors have also joined us as believers. These people are not "crazy" at all, but in secular terms are all incredibly successful. And, we have many people who are successful in other fields as well, such as people who are successful in business and people who are successful as the owners of enterprises. In that sense we have been "proving the Truth."

In short, what I am explaining is this: "The essence of a human is his or her soul. All people have a soul, and while that soul is in our body when we are living and for a short time after our death, that soul perceives itself as having a human shape, and exists as a 'spirit body.' But as time passes, the soul begins to perceive itself not in the shape of a human body, but as an 'energy body' that thinks and feels. This thinking, feeling energy body is what we call a 'spirit,' and the central core of this spirit body is what we call 'the mind'."

An explanation of the "soul"
From a Shinto perspective

As a result of various researches, a number of different religions assert that there are a lot of different elements within this "mind" and that, just as there are fluctuations in people's emotions, the "mind" also has a multi-layered structure. For example, Japanese Shinto does not think of the human soul as being simply one unchanging entity, and proposes that humans are made up of multiple structures.

They say, for example, that there is a soul that expresses happiness, called the *saki-mitama*. This is the soul that represents a human feeling happy. And, there is also the *ara-mitama*, which is the brave aspect of a soul that arises when handing out punishment or engage in combat, like a war god.

Also, there is the spirit of harmony called the *nigi-mitama*. It is focused on bringing harmony, like Amaterasu-O-Mikami, the Sun Goddess. This is the harmonious soul that expresses the traditional Japanese spirit of harmony as seen in rituals like the tea ceremony and *ikebana*, the art of flower arrangement, the harmony of Yamato, the spirit of harmony. Furthermore, there is the *kushi-mitama* soul that expresses the wondrous and mysterious aspects of the soul.

To explain the kushi-mitama further, Japanese Shinto teaches that the soul of human beings has aspects of transformation. We have explored this spiritually in Happy Science as well. It is also recorded in the philosophy of Plato, and the idea is that each type of animal has a soul, and each is symbolic of some kind of mental state.

For example, the lion symbolizes courage, the snake symbolizes cold-blooded cruelty and cunning, while the dove symbolizes peace and the swan symbolizes a soul without impurity. In this way, Plato also talks about how the character of the soul is imprinted in each type of animal.

In other words, the soul of a human can also display similar tendencies to certain types of animals. So there are souls that retain similar tendencies to the tiger, lion, or snake, or the soul of someone who often deceives others in crimes such as fraud has tendencies similar to those of foxes or raccoons.

So, within the idea of kushi-mitama, there is a way of looking at souls from the perspective that "if this soul were to transform into an animal, what would it look like?" I presume that these are the forms that psychics actually saw in the past.

Or, entities that are close to God may appear as forms that have a fair amount of divine power. The four deities who protect Kyoto, one from each direction, are examples of this. A feng shui [geomancy oriented] or Taoist way of thought postulates that these deities transform themselves into dragons or tigers, like the Azure Dragon or the White Tiger, and protect the capital of Japan by taking different forms.

There are examples of this kind of transformation, where a deity transforms into a creature, as well as transformations at the level of ordinary animals. And within the history of Japanese Shinto, such transformations occur in the idea of the kushi-mitama soul.

How does Happy Science understand the "soul"?

As a result of research at Happy Science, we have found that while the souls from a person's past life exist with the individuality that person had when he or she was living with a name, this is not all there is to a soul.

In other words, the soul of a human being exists as a large energy body that can be compared to a bread dough. And just as we can make small bread rolls from that, we form smaller "branch spirits" that can fit into a human body. These are born on earth and possess individuality.

When we are born on the earth, we are born as a man or a woman and this results in our gender characteristics. Or we adopt ways of thinking in line with the job training we undertake in this world. Our awareness of a male or female sense of identity is formed through the soul training we undergo in this world in a physical body. And we retain that sense of awareness in the other world as well.

This being said, we know that among soul groups, some consist of entirely male souls, other groups have only experienced being female, and yet others have both genders. This is one reason why there are some women who, though they possess the outward appearance of a woman, are inwardly tough and strong in a masculine way and excel at masculine tasks.

And it also accounts for why there are some men who, though they possess the outward appearance of a man, are inwardly feminine and are generally called "herbivore men."

In any case, the reason why we are born into this world is to gain "individuality" like pinching off a piece of that bread dough and putting a human body in that piece. We go through life experiences for a number of decades, all for the purpose of attaining that individuality. And until we are reborn and experience the next life, this individuality continues in the Spirit World as well.

An explanation of the Happy Science concept of The theory of "soul siblings"

As I said, a portion of the large spirit body branches off into about six pieces. It is generally thought that most people are made up of about six soul pieces. This line of thought proposes that these six pieces are actually different and discrete beings, and though each experiences life as an individual, the overall assemblage is one comprehensive unit. This is, of course, extremely difficult to grasp in the three-dimensional world we live in.

For example, you can think about it in terms of chemical formulas. If you want to make a bonding formula, you link together various chemical elements to form a unified compound substance. And, in the same way, for a soul to form, multiple elements stick together to form a whole.

Another metaphor that makes this concept easier to grasp in terms of the material world, is the image of a watermill in a stream. The entire structure of the watermill represents the "overall soul."

When a portion of the watermill scoops up the water in the stream, the scooping part of the watermill takes in water and carries it upward, only for it to flow back down into the stream again. The part of the watermill that is in the stream is "the soul in this world." Part of the watermill is in the stream, but the entire watermill is not. And obviously, the watermill itself never leaves the stream entirely. Part of it is always in the stream.

In this way, a portion of the water wheel dips into the water, and it is turned by the flow of the water heading downstream, making the watermill appear alive.

In other words, the part in the water is the "phenomenal world" that is called "this world," or the "three-dimensional world." And the upper part, which is not in the water, is the heavenly world, which is called "the Real

World." So you can see how the parts of a watermill are finely differentiated.

Then, why is part of the watermill made in such a way as to dip into the water to turn the wheels in the mill? The reason why it is made to continue operating as if it were alive is that the power obtained from the rotation, the torque, is applied to something else, for example, it is converted into the power to grind wheat in a mill.

The rotation generates torque to grind wheat with a stone mortar, the energy in the flow of river water is converted into energy to grind wheat and soybeans, and people are able to produce powder without using manpower. So the task or job of milling flour is performed using that rotational power. This is one metaphor for life.

In this way, the essential nature of a human is the "soul." In a broader sense, this nature is a portion of the spiritual entity, or the spirit body, and it takes a human form. This form is not the entirety, but rather, the soul has a number of parts.

And, regarding the part of the soul that is not in this world, the part that remains in the heavenly world, I call that "the subconscious." For example, in psychology, there is an assertion that we do things subconsciously even though we do not think about them with our surface consciousness. This is an example of the influence of the part of our soul that remains in the heavenly world.

What I call "the mind" is the core of the soul. And in actuality, souls exist as groups, and the structure of the soul for most ordinary people is made up of the individual components of about six entities.

High dimensional spirits create souls of Human shape through a "spectrum" of light

As the level of the soul rises to the upper dimensions, from what we call the three-dimensional world to the fourth dimension, the fifth, sixth, seventh, eighth, and to the ninth[*], the total soul energy increases. That is

---

[*] For more details, please refer to *The Nine Dimensions* (New York: IRH Press, 2012), and *Spiritual World 101* (New York: IRH Press, 2015).

because the soul is getting closer to the Being that is called God. As the total energy increases, the example of the watermill no longer fits. It is not a size that can be compared to a bread dough; the soul has a much, much larger amount of energy.

When it comes to the level of a soul that has enough energy to save the human race, that kind of huge soul, that kind of powerful and ancient soul, does not undergo the simple reincarnation of the "core spirit" and the "branch spirit." Instead, a portion of the light is separated out to form a piece out of the large soul.

For example, the portion that is separated out of a large spirit body corresponds to a "portion of a bread dough" which I mentioned earlier, and from that, yet smaller "bread rolls" can be formed. This is the form of high-level soul entities.

Basically, as the soul proceeds upwards, it becomes the essence of a formless energy body itself, and the only question would be how big the total energy body is. That is the structure of the Spirit World.

"The mind" is the central portion
That steers the soul

As a definition, we can say, "A human-shaped soul exists within the large spirit body structure, as a thinking and feeling energy body, and that which exists at the center and 'steers the soul' is the human mind."

Here I must add that the workings of the mind do not equal the functioning of the brain. Actually, what we call "the brain" merely functions like a computer, and it is "the mind" that uses the brain to carry out many different kinds of actions through our physical bodies.

For example, when the brain is damaged, many things can happen, like losing the ability to think, losing the ability to do certain tasks, losing the ability to perform calculations, or losing the ability to speak. However, this is not because the mind is the same as the brain and has been damaged, but instead because, even if you attempt to express a function of your mind, the function of your brain breaks down and the "circuit" between your mind and brain stops operating, causing a "malfunction."

Sometimes its "restoration" is possible through medical intervention, but this attempt is not enough. I teach that even if the body is damaged, even if the brain is damaged, the mind or the soul itself remains healthy.

For example, at Happy Science we have a support movement for disabled children named "You are an angel!" [See back page.] Even if what we see outwardly is a disabled child, even if a child has a different type of body from normal, healthy children, the child's soul is healthy, and the child's mind is normal. It is just that the child cannot move like other normal people, but his or her soul still hears normally.

This is exactly like Helen Keller before she understood the world. If you only saw her acting out of control as a child, you would probably have thought of her as a child who had lost her mind. However, her teacher Anne Sullivan understood that she was acting out because she could not understand language and could not fulfill her natural desire to learn about things, and thus Anne was able to teach her.

For example, she put Helen Keller's hand in cold water and taught her the spelling of "water" until Helen Keller understood "this is water." Once Helen Keller understood it, her soul, her mind became satisfied with learning and knowing.

And as her desire to know was increasingly fulfilled, she eventually became an intelligent person, able to make judgments on her own, and able to think calmly. Although she had been wild before that desire was fulfilled, there was no basic problem with her functioning, and her soul was normal and healthy.

In that sense, a completely healthy human being is a miraculous occurrence wherein both the soul and the physical body are perfectly linked to operate together.

The Buddhist understanding
Of "the mind"

Speaking in Buddhist terms, of course analysis of the mind becomes an even more detailed discussion. In general, scholars of medical science, biology, and physiology in this world tend to see things with a focus on awareness through the sensory organs.

Buddhism also acknowledges the existence of the power to recognize the different objects of this world through the five sense-organs, and this is made up of the five aggregates of "all forms of matter, perception, mental conceptions and ideas, volition, and consciousness of mind."

However, the teachings of Buddhism assert that these are merely sensations received through the physical body, and that it would be wrong to think that these represent your mind.

For example, the first element is "all forms of matter," meaning material things. We understand these material things through information that comes to us through our visual and auditory senses. That is "perception," the second element.

Then we go through a mental operation of "thinking" about what we perceive, and this is "mental conceptions and ideas." Then we engage in "volition" based on those thoughts, resulting in our reaction and action. And recognizing the results of this is called "consciousness of the mind." This is the explanation of "all forms of matter, perception, mental conceptions and ideas, volition, and consciousness of mind."

However, it would be wrong to mistake what occurs through the reaction of these physical sensory organs as ourselves, to think of those reactions as being who we are. All of them will eventually fade away according to the principle of "the impermanence of all things." All phenomena are non-ego, and every living thing will eventually die, lose its cohesion, become ashes or soil, and fade away. Sensory organs based in the physical body all eventually fade away, and we are left with the truth that, "this is not your true nature after all."

In fact, your true nature does not lie in these five sense-organs but transcends them. This true nature which transcends those sensory organs is the part that corresponds to the center of "the mind." In Sanskrit it is called *manas*, and from ancient times this has traditionally been taught in Buddhism.

Although it is not easy to fully comprehend such a religious explanation, I have attempted to address the question of "what is the mind" in a straightforward way.

Afterword

Analyzing the current state of affairs of religion and religious universities in Japan, and looking at the way religion is generally treated in universities in this nation, it seems as if "academic freedom" and "religious freedom" are two completely incompatible concepts.

Happy Science Group already operates the Happy Science Academy Junior and Senior High Schools in two locations. These schools have demonstrated achievements to the level where they are recognized as model schools in Tochigi Prefecture and Shiga Prefecture, both as schools with a track record for excellence in the athletics and culture departments, as well as for academic disciplines.

Many principals and vice principals visit our schools, saying, "Tell us how your schools have come to be so amazing." They are so impressed that they ask us to give model lessons at their schools. All of this is the result of new religious education and has been made possible through the development of excellent educational materials and methods.

It is our dream to <u>spark Zeitgeist [the spirit of a new age]</u> <u>through a university as well,</u> to become the driving force to achieve a reformation of university education in Japan, and prove ourselves to be <u>a model school for the entire</u> <u>world</u>. We sincerely ask for the support and approval of the people of Japan and the entire world.

Ryuho Okawa
Founder and CEO of Happy Science Group
Founder of Happy Science University
August 16, 2014

ABOUT THE AUTHOR

Founder and CEO of Happy Science Group.

Ryuho Okawa was born on July 7th 1956, in Tokushima, Japan. After graduating from the University of Tokyo with a law degree, he joined a Tokyo-based trading house. While working at its New York headquarters, he studied international finance at the Graduate Center of the City University of New York. In 1981, he attained Great Enlightenment and became aware that he is El Cantare with a mission to bring salvation to all humankind.

In 1986, he established Happy Science. It now has members in over 165 countries across the world, with more than 700 branches and temples as well as 10,000 missionary houses around the world.

He has given over 3,450 lectures (of which more than 150 are in English) and published over 3,000 books (of which more than 600 are Spiritual Interview Series), and many are translated into 40 languages. Along with *The Laws of the Sun* and *The Laws Of Messiah*, many of the books have become best sellers or million sellers. To date, Happy Science has produced 25 movies. The original story and original concept were given by the Executive Producer Ryuho Okawa. He has also composed music and written lyrics of over 450 pieces.

Moreover, he is the Founder of Happy Science University and Happy Science Academy (Junior and Senior High School), Founder and President of the Happiness Realization Party, Founder and Honorary Headmaster of Happy Science Institute of Government and Management, Founder of IRH Press Co., Ltd., and the Chairperson of NEW STAR PRODUCTION Co., Ltd. and ARI Production Co., Ltd.

WHAT IS EL CANTARE?

El Cantare means "the Light of the Earth," and is the Supreme God of the Earth who has been guiding humankind since the beginning of Genesis. He is whom Jesus called Father and Muhammad called Allah, and is *Ame-no-Mioya-Gami*, Japanese Father God. Different parts of El Cantare's core consciousness have descended to Earth in the past, once as Alpha and another as Elohim. His branch spirits, such as Shakyamuni Buddha and Hermes, have descended to Earth many times and helped to flourish many civilizations. To unite various religions and to integrate various fields of study in order to build a new civilization on Earth, a part of the core consciousness has descended to Earth as Master Ryuho Okawa.

Alpha is a part of the core consciousness of El Cantare who descended to Earth around 330 million years ago. Alpha preached Earth's Truths to harmonize and unify Earth-born humans and space people who came from other planets.

Elohim is a part of El Cantare's core consciousness who descended to Earth around 150 million years ago. He gave wisdom, mainly on the differences of light and darkness, good and evil.

Ame-no-Mioya-Gami (Japanese Father God) is the Creator God and the Father God who appears in the ancient literature, *Hotsuma Tsutae*. It is believed that He descended on the foothills of Mt. Fuji about 30,000 years ago and built the Fuji dynasty, which is the root of the Japanese civilization. With justice as the central pillar, Ame-no-Mioya-Gami's teachings spread to ancient civilizations of other countries in the world.

Shakyamuni Buddha was born as a prince into the Shakya Clan in India around 2,600 years ago. When he was 29 years old, he renounced the world and sought enlightenment. He later attained Great Enlightenment and founded Buddhism.

Hermes is one of the 12 Olympian gods in Greek mythology, but the spiritual Truth is that he taught the teachings of love and progress around 4,300 years ago that became the origin of the current Western civilization. He is a hero that truly existed.

Ophealis was born in Greece around 6,500 years ago and was the leader who took an expedition to as far as Egypt. He is the God of miracles, prosperity, and arts, and is known as Osiris in the Egyptian mythology.

Rient Arl Croud was born as a king of the ancient Incan Empire around 7,000 years ago and taught about the mysteries of the mind. In the heavenly world, he is responsible for the interactions that take place between various planets.

Thoth was an almighty leader who built the golden age of the Atlantic civilization around 12,000 years ago. In the Egyptian mythology, he is known as god Thoth.

Ra Mu was a leader who built the golden age of the civilization of Mu around 17,000 years ago. As a religious leader and a politician, he ruled by uniting religion and politics.

ABOUT HAPPY SCIENCE

Happy Science is a global movement that empowers individuals to find purpose and spiritual happiness and to share that happiness with their families, societies, and the world. With more than 12 million members around the world, Happy Science aims to increase awareness of spiritual truths and expand our capacity for love, compassion, and joy so that together we can create the kind of world we all wish to live in.

Activities at Happy Science are based on the Principle of Happiness (Love, Wisdom, Self-Reflection, and Progress). This principle embraces worldwide philosophies and beliefs, transcending boundaries of culture and religions.

Love teaches us to give ourselves freely without expecting anything in return; it encompasses giving, nurturing, and forgiving.

Wisdom leads us to the insights of spiritual truths, and opens us to the true meaning of life and the will of God (the universe, the highest power, Buddha).

Self-Reflection brings a mindful, nonjudgmental lens to our thoughts and actions to help us find our truest selves—the essence of our souls—and deepen our connection to the highest power. It helps us attain a clean and peaceful mind and leads us to the right life path.

Progress emphasizes the positive, dynamic aspects of our spiritual growth—actions we can take to manifest and spread happiness around the world. It's a path that not only expands our soul growth, but also furthers the collective potential of the world we live in.

PROGRAMS AND EVENTS

The doors of Happy Science are open to all. We offer a variety of programs and events, including self-exploration and self-growth programs, spiritual seminars, meditation and contemplation sessions, study groups, and book events.

Our programs are designed to:
* Deepen your understanding of your purpose and meaning in life
* Improve your relationships and increase your capacity to love unconditionally
* Attain peace of mind, decrease anxiety and stress, and feel positive
* Gain deeper insights and a broader perspective on the world
* Learn how to overcome life's challenges
   ... and much more.

For more information, visit happy-science.org.

OUR ACTIVITIES

Happy Science does other various activities to provide support for those in need.

◆ **You Are An Angel! General Incorporated Association**

Happy Science has a volunteer network in Japan that encourages and supports children with disabilities as well as their parents and guardians.

◆ **Never Mind School for Truancy**

At 'Never Mind,' we support students who find it very challenging to attend schools in Japan. We also nurture their self-help spirit and power to rebound against obstacles in life based on Master Okawa's teachings and faith.

◆ **"Prevention Against Suicide" Campaign since 2003**

A nationwide campaign to reduce suicides; over 20,000 people commit suicide every year in Japan. "The Suicide Prevention Website-Words of Truth for You-" presents spiritual prescriptions for worries such as depression, lost love, extramarital affairs, bullying and work-related problems, thereby saving many lives.

◆ **Support for Anti-bullying Campaigns**

Happy Science provides support for a group of parents and guardians, Network to Protect Children from Bullying, a general incorporated foundation launched in Japan to end bullying, including those that can even be called a criminal offense. So far, the network received more than 5,000 cases and resolved 90% of them.

- **The Golden Age Scholarship**

  This scholarship is granted to students who can contribute greatly and bring a hopeful future to the world.

- **Success No.1**
  Buddha's Truth Afterschool Academy

  Happy Science has over 180 classrooms throughout Japan and in several cities around the world that focus on afterschool education for children. The education focuses on faith and morals in addition to supporting children's school studies.

- **Angel Plan V**

  For children under the age of kindergarten, Happy Science holds classes for nurturing healthy, positive, and creative boys and girls.

- **Future Stars Training Department**

  The Future Stars Training Department was founded within the Happy Science Media Division with the goal of nurturing talented individuals to become successful in the performing arts and entertainment industry.

- **NEW STAR PRODUCTION Co., Ltd.**
  ARI Production Co., Ltd.

  We have companies to nurture actors and actresses, artists, and vocalists. They are also involved in film production.

CONTACT INFORMATION

Happy Science is a worldwide organization with branches and temples around the globe. For a comprehensive list, visit the worldwide directory at *happy-science.org*. The following are some of the many Happy Science locations:

UNITED STATES AND CANADA

New York
79 Franklin St., New York, NY 10013, USA
Phone: 1-212-343-7972
Fax: 1-212-343-7973
Email: ny@happy-science.org
Website: happyscience-usa.org

New Jersey
66 Hudson St., #2R, Hoboken, NJ 07030, USA
Phone: 1-201-313-0127
Email: nj@happy-science.org
Website: happyscience-usa.org

Chicago
2300 Barrington Rd., Suite #400,
Hoffman Estates, IL 60169, USA
Phone: 1-630-937-3077
Email: chicago@happy-science.org
Website: happyscience-usa.org

Florida
5208 8th St., Zephyrhills, FL 33542, USA
Phone: 1-813-715-0000
Fax: 1-813-715-0010
Email: florida@happy-science.org
Website: happyscience-usa.org

Atlanta
1874 Piedmont Ave., NE Suite 360-C
Atlanta, GA 30324, USA
Phone: 1-404-892-7770
Email: atlanta@happy-science.org
Website: happyscience-usa.org

San Francisco
525 Clinton St.
Redwood City, CA 94062, USA
Phone & Fax: 1-650-363-2777
Email: sf@happy-science.org
Website: happyscience-usa.org

Los Angeles
1590 E. Del Mar Blvd., Pasadena, CA
91106, USA
Phone: 1-626-395-7775
Fax: 1-626-395-7776
Email: la@happy-science.org
Website: happyscience-usa.org

Orange County
16541 Gothard St. Suite 104
Huntington Beach, CA 92647
Phone: 1-714-659-1501
Email: oc@happy-science.org
Website: happyscience-usa.org

San Diego
7841 Balboa Ave. Suite #202
San Diego, CA 92111, USA
Phone: 1-626-395-7775
Fax: 1-626-395-7776
E-mail: sandiego@happy-science.org
Website: happyscience-usa.org

Hawaii
Phone: 1-808-591-9772
Fax: 1-808-591-9776
Email: hi@happy-science.org
Website: happyscience-usa.org

Kauai
3343 Kanakolu Street, Suite 5
Lihue, HI 96766, USA
Phone: 1-808-822-7007
Fax: 1-808-822-6007
Email: kauai-hi@happy-science.org
Website: happyscience-usa.org

Toronto

845 The Queensway
Etobicoke, ON M8Z 1N6, Canada
Phone: 1-416-901-3747
Email: toronto@happy-science.org
Website: happy-science.ca

Vancouver

#201-2607 East 49th Avenue,
Vancouver, BC, V5S 1J9, Canada
Phone: 1-604-437-7735
Fax: 1-604-437-7764
Email: vancouver@happy-science.org
Website: happy-science.ca

INTERNATIONAL

Tokyo

1-6-7 Togoshi, Shinagawa,
Tokyo, 142-0041, Japan
Phone: 81-3-6384-5770
Fax: 81-3-6384-5776
Email: tokyo@happy-science.org
Website: happy-science.org

Seoul

74, Sadang-ro 27-gil,
Dong ak-gu, Seoul, Korea
Phone: 82-2-3478-8777
Fax: 82-2-3478-9777
Email: korea@happy-science.org
Website: happyscience-korea.org

London

3 Margaret St.
London, W1W 8RE United Kingdom
Phone: 44-20-7323-9255
Fax: 44-20-7323-9344
Email: eu@happy-science.org
Website: www.happyscience-uk.org

Taipei

No. 89, Lane 155, Dunhua N. Road,
Songshan District, Taipei City 105, Taiwan
Phone 886-2-2719-9377
Fax: 886-2-2719-5570
Email: taiwan@happy-science.org
Website: happyscience-tw.org

Sydney

516 Pacific Highway, Lane Cove North,
2066 NSW, Australia
Phone: 61-2-9411-2877
Fax: 61-2-9411-2822
Email: sydney@happy-science.org

Kuala Lumpur

No 22A, Block 2, Jalil Link Jalan Jalil
Jaya 2, Bukit Jalil 57000,
Kuala Lumpur, Malaysia
Phone: 60-3-8998-7877
Fax: 60-3-8998-7977
Email: malaysia@happy-science.org
Website: happyscience.org.my

Sao Paulo

Rua. Domingos de Morais 1154,
Vila Mariana, Sao Paulo SP
CEP 04010-100, Brazil
Phone: 55-11-5088-3800
Email: sp@happy-science.org
Website: happyscience.com.br

Kathmandu

Kathmandu Metropolitan City,
Ward No. 15, Ring Road, Kimdol,
Sitapaila Kathmardu, Nepal
Phone: 977-1-427-2931
Email: nepal@happy-science.org

Jundiai

Rua Congo, 447, Jd. Bonfiglioli
Jundiai-CEP, 13207-340, Brazil
Phone: 55-11-4587-5952
Email: jundiai@happy-science.org

Kampala

Plot 877 Rubaga Road, Kampala
P.O. Box 34130 Kampala, UGANDA
Phone: 256-79-4682-121
Email: uganda@happy-science.org

ABOUT HAPPINESS REALIZATION PARTY

The Happiness Realization Party (HRP) was founded in May 2009 by Master Ryuho Okawa as part of the Happy Science Group. HRP strives to improve the Japanese society, based on three basic political principles of "freedom, democracy, and faith," and let Japan promote individual and public happiness from Asia to the world as a leader nation.

1) Diplomacy and Security: Protecting Freedom, Democracy, and Faith of Japan and the World from China's Totalitarianism

Japan's current defense system is insufficient against China's expanding hegemony and the threat of North Korea's nuclear missiles. Japan, as the leader of Asia, must strengthen its defense power and promote strategic diplomacy together with the nations which share the values of freedom, democracy, and faith. Further, HRP aims to realize world peace under the leadership of Japan, the nation with the spirit of religious tolerance.

2) Economy: Early economic recovery through utilizing the "wisdom of the private sector"

Economy has been damaged severely by the novel coronavirus originated in China. Many companies have been forced into bankruptcy or out of business. What is needed for economic recovery now is not subsidies and regulations by the government, but policies which can utilize the "wisdom of the private sector."

For more information, visit en.hr-party.jp

HAPPY SCIENCE ACADEMY
JUNIOR AND SENIOR HIGH SCHOOL

Happy Science Academy Junior and Senior High School is a boarding school founded with the goal of educating the future leaders of the world who can have a big vision, persevere, and take on new challenges.

Currently, there are two campuses in Japan; the Nasu Main Campus in Tochigi Prefecture, founded in 2010, and the Kansai Campus in Shiga Prefecture, founded in 2013.

Nasu Main Campus

Kansai Campus

# HAPPY SCIENCE UNIVERSITY

THE FOUNDING SPIRIT AND THE GOAL OF EDUCATION

Based on the founding philosophy of the university, "Exploration of happiness and the creation of a new civilization," education, research and studies will be provided to help students acquire deep understanding grounded in religious belief and advanced expertise with the objectives of producing "great talents of virtue" who can contribute in a broad-ranging way to serve Japan and the international society.

FACULTIES

Faculty of human happiness

Students in this faculty will pursue liberal arts from various perspectives with a multidisciplinary approach, explore and envision an ideal state of human beings and society.

Faculty of successful management

This faculty aims to realize successful management that helps organizations to create value and wealth for society and to contribute to the happiness and the development of management and employees as well as society as a whole.

Faculty of future creation

Students in this faculty study subjects such as political science, journalism, performing arts and artistic expression, and explore and present new political and cultural models based on truth, goodness and beauty.

Faculty of future industry

This faculty aims to nurture engineers who can resolve various issues facing modern civilization from a technological standpoint and contribute to the creation of new industries of the future.

ABOUT HS PRESS

HS Press is an imprint of IRH Press Co., Ltd. IRH Press Co., Ltd., based in Tokyo, was founded in 1987 as a publishing division of Happy Science. IRH Press publishes religious and spiritual books, journals, magazines and also operates broadcast and film production enterprises. For more information, visit *okawabooks.com*.

Follow us on:

f Facebook: Okawa Books   Instagram: OkawaBooks
▶ Youtube: Okawa Books   Twitter: Okawa Books
𝓟 Pinterest: Okawa Books   Goodreads: Ryuho Okawa

———— **NEWSLETTER** ————

To receive book related news, promotions and events, please subscribe to our newsletter below.

⌀ eepurl.com/bsMeJj

 ———— **AUDIO / VISUAL MEDIA** ————

YOUTUBE   **PODCAST**

Introduction of Ryuho Okawa's titles; topics ranging from self-help, current affairs, spirituality, religion, and the universe.

BOOKS BY RYUHO OKAWA

THE LAWS OF WISDOM
SHINE YOUR DIAMOND WITHIN

This book guides you along the path on how to acquire wisdom, so that you can break through any wall you are facing or will confront in your life or in your business. You will lean how to go beyond the level of just amassing knowledge. It will help you come up with many great ideas, make effective planning and strategy and develop your leadership skills.

THE LAWS OF PERSEVERANCE
REVERSING YOUR COMMON SENSE

"No matter how much you suffer, the Truth will gradually shine forth as you continue to endure hardships. Therefore, simply strengthen your mind and keep making constant efforts in times of endurance, however ordinary they may be. "

-From the Postscript

THE LAWS OF GREAT ENLIGHTENMENT
ALWAYS WALK WITH BUDDHA

We often find ourselves unable to forgive someone and maintain a peaceful mind. However, there are ways to lead a stress-free life and enjoy happiness from within. By understanding the Buddhist concept of "enlightenment" in this book, you will gain the power to forgive sins and get to know how to be the master of your own mind.

For a complete list of books, visit okawabooks.com

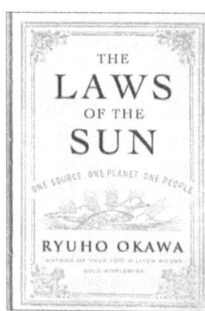

THE LAWS OF THE SUN

ONE SOURCE, ONE PLANET, ONE PEOPLE

Imagine if you could ask God why He created this world and what spiritual laws He used to shape us—and everything around us. If we could understand His designs and intentions, we could discover what our goals in life should be and whether our actions move us closer to those goals or farther away.

THE GOLDEN LAWS

HISTORY THROUGH THE EYES OF THE ETERNAL BUDDHA

The Golden Laws reveals how Buddha's Plan has been unfolding on earth, and outlines five thousand years of the secret history of humankind. Once we understand the true course of history, we cannot help but become aware of the significance of our spiritual mission in the present age.

THE NINE DIMENSIONS

UNVEILING THE LAWS OF ETERNITY

This book is a window into the mind of our loving God, who encourages us to grow into greater angels. It reveals His deepest intentions, answering the timely question of why He conceived such a colorful medley of religions, philosophies, sciences, arts, and other forms of expression.

For a complete list of books, visit okawabooks.com

The New Idea of a University

The Groundbreaking Mission of Happy Science University

In this book, Ryuho Okawa, the author and founder of Happy Science University, shares his vision for Happy Science University, a new type of university that has no equivalent anywhere in the world. This groundbreaking philosophy will provide unique values to the existing academic world and greatly advance the function and the role of universities in society. *The New Idea of a University* is a book that opens new frontiers of academia and that provides clear guidelines for leading the world into a better future.

The Basic Teachings of Happy Science

A Happiness Theory on Truth and Faith

In this book, it can be said that the author has given us the basic teachings of Happy Science that are continuously evolving and developing, in light of the vast amount of teachings from the 1800 books, but from a completely different angle using new words. When you finish reading this book, three key words, Truth, Faith and Mission that are indispensable to achieve happiness will be left in your heart, and you are bound to discover yourself filled with the wish to live a life of Truth.

For a complete list of books, visit okawabooks.com

MUSIC BY RYUHO OKAWA

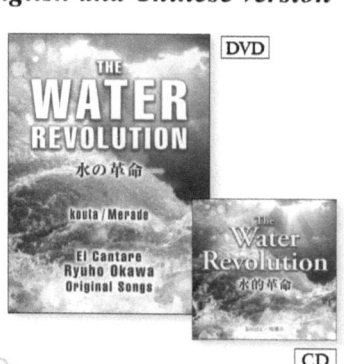

With Savior *English version*

DVD

CD

This is the message of hope to the modern people who are living in the midst of the Coronavirus pandemic, natural disasters, economic depression, and other various crises.

Search on YouTube

with savior for a short ad!

The Thunder

a composition for repelling the Coronavirus

We have been granted this music from our Lord. It will repel away the novel Coronavirus originated in China. Experience this magnificent powerful music.

Search on YouTube

the thunder composition

for a short ad!

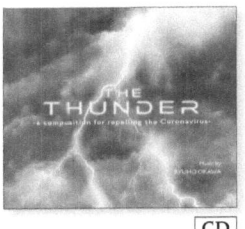

CD

The Exorcism

prayer music for repelling Lost Spirits

CD

Feel the divine vibrations of this Japanese and Western exorcising symphony to banish all evil possessions you suffer from and to purify your space!

Search on YouTube

the exorcism repelling

for a short ad!

119